Six Ways To Enjoy This S[...]

Text **60 Minutes**	The length of our small books is based on the time in the air of a flight between Toronto and Chicago. Start reading as you take off and finish the book by the time you land. Just the right length for the 21st-century reader.
Cartoons **30 Minutes**	You can also gain a complete overview of the ideas in this book by looking at the cartoons and reading the captions. We find the cartoons have made our Strategic Coach concepts accessible to readers as young as eight years old.
Audio **120 Minutes**	The audio recording that accompanies this book is not just a recitation of the printed words but an in-depth commentary that expands each chapter's mindset into new dimensions. Download the audio at **strategiccoach.com/go/otlagd**
Video **30 Minutes**	Our video interviews about the concepts in the book deepen your understanding of the mindsets. If you combine text, cartoons, audio, and video, your understanding of the ideas will be 10x greater than you would gain from reading only. Watch the videos at **strategiccoach.com/go/otlagd**
Scorecard **10 Minutes**	Score your "Owning Technology" mindset at **strategiccoach.com/go/otlagd**. First, score yourself on where you are now, and then fill in where you want to be a year from now.
ebook **1 Minute**	After absorbing the fundamental ideas of the "Owning Technology" concept, you can quickly and easily share them by sending the ebook version to as many other individuals as you desire. Direct them to **strategiccoach.com/go/otlagd**

Thanks to the Creative Team:

Adam Morrison

Kerri Morrison

Hamish MacDonald

Shannon Waller

Jennifer Bhatthal

Margaux Yiu

Suvi Siu

Christine Nishino

Willard Bond

Peggy Lam

Alex Varley

Owning Technology Like A Great Dog

Dogs thrive when they can make sense of the rules and the relationships around them. Likewise, technology is an amazing companion when you give it a role to play, but it will drive you crazy and make a mess if you think it's in charge.

You own technology—not the other way around. And only the technologies that are useful to you should be a part of your life. Adopt the eight ownership mindsets in this book to ensure a positive relationship with both dogs and technology.

Cartoons by Hamish MacDonald.

Printed in Toronto, Canada. The Strategic Coach Inc., 33 Fraser Avenue, Suite 201, Toronto, Ontario, M6K 3J9.

This publication is meant to strengthen your common sense, not to substitute for it. It is also not a substitute for the advice of your doctor, lawyer, accountant, or any of your advisors, personal or professional.

If you would like further information about The Strategic Coach® Program or other Strategic Coach® services and products, please telephone 416.531.7399 or 1.800.387.3206.

Library and Archives Canada Cataloguing in Publication

Title: Owning technology like a great dog : always remember you're in charge / Dan Sullivan ;
    cartoons by Hamish MacDonald.

Names: Sullivan, Dan, 1944- author.

Identifiers: Canadiana 20230505945 | ISBN 9781897239865 (softcover)

Subjects: LCSH: Business—Data processing. | LCSH: Employees—Effect of technological innovations on.
    | LCSH: Business enterprises—Technological innovations. | LCSH: Business enterprises—Computer
    networks. | LCSH: Success in business.

Classification: LCC HF5548.2 .S87 2023 | DDC 658/.05—dc23

Contents

Introduction
Being A Great Owner

You're an increasingly talented and successful achiever, and every useful technology supports your best progress and growth.

You can tell a lot about a person by their relationship with dogs, and, likewise, you can tell a lot about a person by their relationship with technology.

Great dogs already demonstrate how all of your existing and future technology can be trained. Great dogs are those who understand that you're the owner in all situations and activities. In the same way, you should be the leader in your relationship with all existing and future technology.

There are eight ways you can be an increasingly great leader and trainer in all of your ongoing interactions with any kind of technology—any device, process, system, or network—now and in your future. You're always the enterprising owner, and useful technology supports your progress.

You'll only have a satisfying relationship with dogs if you establish that you're the owner. You have to be the leader in that relationship. How you treat yourself as a human determines whether you have a good relationship with dogs and whether you have a good relationship with technology.

30,000-year technology.
Humans have been productively teaming up with dogs since long before recorded history, perhaps as long as 30,000 years ago when dogs split from their wolf ancestors. After taming and utilizing fire, training dogs was our next greatest "technological" jump.

Human beings recognized how we could benefit from what dogs are able to do. This included hunting and protection.

As an achiever, I want to get a lot done, and I want to experience a lot of success. So with everything I encounter, I want to figure out how that technology, person, or animal can support my being an achiever.

Teamwork with dogs.

Long ago, there were a few canny wolves who teamed up with enterprising humans to create a new joint capability called "dogs." For both wolves and humans, this teamwork has created enormous advantages ever since.

Dogs are problem solvers. They'll try to solve a problem, and if they can't solve it, they'll come to a human to solve it for them. In our relationship with dogs, we benefit from what they do, and they rely on us to do the things they can't.

It's impossible to know for certain how this teamwork first came about. It could even be that it was discovered accidentally. But something we know for certain is that our teamwork with dogs is remarkable. We know how they can support and assist us in what we want, and they seem to recognize that we can make things happen that are beyond their abilities.

Dogs need a caring owner.

Dogs are interactive social animals who require a responsible leader who gives them useful direction. With a bad owner, this is missing. In teamwork with us, dogs need a caring human to reinforce their best behavior.

When it comes to dogs, their good behavior comes from guidance and positive reinforcement from their owner. And their bad behavior comes from being confused—unless they were trained to behave badly, which is a different story. If you establish yourself as a kind leader in your relationship with your dog, you'll get the behavior you desire from them.

The same is true for technology if you recognize that you, and not it, are in charge. You can train technology to do what you want and only what you want.

The technology is only as useful as you are. It acts as a magnifier. You can see how this works by going on social media. People who aren't useful to themselves or others don't become useful by using the technology. They just project their unhappiness out into the world, often by attacking other people.

But if you're already a useful person who provides value, technology can amplify your capabilities and impact.

Taming technology.

There's growing confusion in today's world due to constant technological innovation—so many devices, so much complexity. Like packs of dangerous wolves! But you can simplify it all by training your technology. Like a great dog.

It's not about the dog or the technology—it's about you. Just as you have to train yourself to be a leader with dogs, you have to train yourself to be a leader with technology. If you do this, the resulting teamwork will be extraordinary.

You'll be able to use technology to expand your freedoms of time, money, relationship, and purpose. You'll reinforce your ability to commit to projects, be courageous in creating something new, develop new capabilities, and increase your confidence. The payoffs for training technology like a great dog are growth and progress.

Eight "great owner" mindsets.

There are eight ways of thinking about being a great owner for all of your technological "dogs." The moment you begin mastering these mindsets, your command of useful technology will multiply:

1. Liking who you are.
2. Loving what you have.
3. Strengthening your talent.
4. Deepening your values.
5. Increasing your usefulness.
6. Multiplying your impact.
7. Reversing your aging.
8. Slowing life down.

You're in charge. And the more you engage with technology using the eight mindsets we'll explore in depth in this book, the more you'll increase your impact, grow your innovation, and feel that you're in control of technology rather than the other way around.

Chapter 1
Mindset 1: Liking Who You Are

You're always expanding your best self — what you do uniquely well — and you create your greatest value for other great people.

Dogs are frequently referred to as "man's best friend." This is true even when the humans don't deserve it. Even when mean and nasty people train their dogs to be vicious, the dogs, strangely, still tend to love their human owners. There's a lot to learn from this, but the better approach for you is to make it easier for the outside world—dogs and people—to automatically like you and everything you do.

This is simple: Always be liking yourself to start with. When it comes to your use of technology, every way you use it will have a "likable" impact that will continually multiply going forward.

Dogs want to please you, but if you're not pleased with yourself, it's very hard for them. Dogs pick up emotionally on who you are in relationship to yourself, and if you don't like yourself, they don't have the sense that you're a leader in your relationship with them. But people who have good relationships with dogs tend to become nicer people. And taking responsibility for being a good owner tends to make you like yourself better.

Expanding your best self.

You're always improving yourself today by comparing yourself to your previous best self. As you progress, you like who you are even more than you did a year ago. Looking forward, you always have a clear-cut, achievable, and measurable vision where your best self is bigger. New technology can support this.

I liked my best self when I was eight, I liked my best self when I was 20, I liked my best self when I was 40, and I like my best self now. Every time I jump to a new level, I'm more capable and more engaged in a creative and productive way with the world.

But I like who I was when I wasn't as creative and productive because I was the best I could be at that time. There's nothing I could have done back then to be better. There's no reason to beat yourself up for how you were in the past. You're always at 100 percent. But the 100 percent gets bigger. And you're always using new technology to make yourself bigger and better.

Past, present, and future uniqueness.

From the start, you've had a unique sense about who you are as well as your own unique ambitions, insights, and skills. Your internal sense of uniqueness is now having a greater external impact. More and more, you're creating unique value in other people's lives. And technology enables you to get the word out around the world.

Technology is a magnifier and a multiplier. It doesn't change something from bad to good or vice versa. It magnifies and multiplies your uniqueness.

Dogs are similar. If you're a great owner, you're going to have a great dog. If you train your dog to be bad, your dog is going to be bad. Their behavior reflects back on you. Just like with technology, the results you get have everything to do with your approach.

Attracting other "best friends."

When you clearly like yourself, dogs will like you 10x more. As an even bigger bonus, the best people will want to be your friends. Like attracts like in every area of human activity around the world. And you live in a technological age when the "best friends" worldwide can collaborate 10x.

From day one, the two main ways of learning have been imitation and repetition. So, we see behavior that other people exhibit that we admire, and then we try to take on that quality inside of ourselves. And then we do it over and over and over again.

Because we have this genetically ingrained ability to imitate what we're attracted to, we have to be very careful who we spend time with. Make sure you're around people who demonstrate creativity, productivity, results, and impact.

Multiplying your greatest value.

People who like themselves make great dog owners. Dogs with likable owners become very useful and skilled if they're trained at continually higher levels.

For yourself, liking who you are when so many other people don't like themselves can often become your greatest value that technology endlessly multiplies.

People who don't like themselves probably haven't liked themselves since childhood. They look at what others have, and they create ideals of who they're going to be in the future. But they're trying to be someone else. It's a complete rejection of who they themselves are right now. There's no growth possible with this kind of person.

Increasing teamwork and collaboration.
Great dog owners in the world have created countless forms of teamwork with great dogs, and the list of surprising new ways keeps growing. It seems there's no upper limit.

And that goes for your teamwork with technology as well. Because you keep liking yourself more, your use of technology will grow and improve, and you'll gain a mastery over it.

Again, what technology does is magnify and multiply what's good or bad. You use it to magnify and multiply your uniqueness, and your uniqueness is something you increasingly like.

A lot of other people use technology in the external world to work out internal issues that they should keep to themselves. Not everything you do should be projected out into the world.

Think of who the target audience is for everything you're considering using technology to multiply. For all of the good stuff you put out, there will be an audience with whom it resonates.

Chapter 2
Mindset 2: Loving What You Have

You continually deepen your appreciation for everything you already have, seeing every new aspect of it as more valuable going forward.

Your relationship with dogs keeps growing because they sense and love that you appreciate them for their companionship and usefulness. But what they continually respond to is that they get to live with you for their whole lives in your overall world that is appreciating in value. It's both deepening in quality and expanding in quantity. You love this world that you're creating, and so do they.

You have a qualitative and quantitative impact on the world. If you have a dog, your appreciating value goes to them too. Dogs know how their owners feel about them, and dogs like being liked. You appreciate your dog, and they feel that. They grow as a result of your appreciation for what they do and who they are.

Technology can't feel emotions or appreciation, but when you appreciate it, you're better at using it. You're more alert and aware about it, and you're better at seeing its impact.

Deepening, expanding awareness.

With you, everything grows more valuable, beautiful, and meaningful, including your dogs. How you look at and treat them continually brings out the best in them. Your awareness of their unique value motivates them to deepen and expand it. And every day, the technology you value multiplies its value for you. It's a reciprocal relationship.

I think of the way that Zoom has become a huge capability for me and for our company. We have a relationship with it, and we've maximized what you can do with it. We can multiply technology's value to us.

I've noticed that oftentimes people want to own new things because they're not happy with what they already have. For them, the pleasure is in the acquisition of new things, and that fades pretty quickly and then they want to acquire more. But true ownership means that you deepen the pleasure and enjoyment you get from what you already own. In order to grow, you have to expand your ownership.

And the more you give space for deepening, expanding awareness, the more you can take ownership over your experience, talents, situations, and responses.

Grateful for what you're creating.
Your whole life seems like a single, unified, expanding experience that you're always in the process of creating. The dogs in your life are very fortunate because you're such a marvelous owner. Experiences that happened years ago seem as fresh as today's.

You've always been creating, and you'll always be creating. You're not appreciating something that you did in the past— you're appreciating a lifelong capability that you have. It's continuous. You're never going to reach a point where you say, "I've had enough of doing this." Creating is what you do. To give up doing what you do would be like give up living your life.

Most people think of 70 as an age at which they'll have retired. I've accomplished more since I turned 70 than I did in my first 70 years of life. This is partly due to the fact that

I've become increasingly attuned to what's going to increase my impact, including technology.

Increasing everything's value.
Because of your growing appreciation for every day's activities, situations, and interactions, you're always raising everything's value—not only for yourself, but also in ways that other people experience.

Appreciation is both an emotional quality and an economic quality. It has two separate meanings: It means gratitude for what you have, and that gratitude also increases the value of what you're grateful for.

When humans began to use dogs as an early form of technology, their appreciation and gratitude for the benefits of their teamwork also increased the dogs' value to them. Everything increases in value to the degree that they're appreciated.

Measuring progress backwards.
The dogs in your life reflect in their behavior what's happening inside of you. Your actual self is expanding so positively that you're never trying to reach unachievable ideals. Rather, you always measure all progress by comparing who you are now with who you were at past starting points.

We can use ideals to illuminate where we want to go, but actually achieving an ideal is impossible. If you measure where you are against an ideal, you'll always fall short. The only real measurements you can get of your progress are from measuring where you are right now back to where you were when you started out. This keeps you in a positive frame of mind where you're always focused on how far you've come.

If you're focused on ideals, that's a sign that you don't like who you are. It's a sign that you want to be someone else.

Always attracting bigger and better.

Because your appreciation of everything and everyone around you continually grows, the world around you returns the favor. Dogs in your life are more excited to see you every morning and strive to grow every day. Your use of existing and new technology is always opening up new and bigger opportunities for you.

You're learning to use technology in the best way because you're learning to think about dogs when you think about technology. When you're approaching a new technology, consider how you would approach a dog. Oftentimes, you might get angry when you're using a technology and things don't go how you want them to. But if you consider the analogy, you wouldn't get angry at a dog. You'd just change the instruction so that you get the result you want. You want to work with technology to get the best out of it, not be fighting against it.

I always say, "Our eyes only see and our ears only hear what our brain is looking for." When you're actively looking for new ways to be useful, you'll come across technology that can help you. If you're scared or closed off, you won't see that. But when you're grounded within yourself and your own creativity and value creation, you can see what's going to multiply it.

Chapter 3
Mindset 3: Strengthening Your Talent
You're clearer and more confident every year about what you do uniquely well that others value most.

And every year, the word goes out further to more individuals who can best utilize your best talents. When it comes to interacting with dogs in your life, they respond extraordinarily well to engaging with you because your best abilities continually improve theirs.

This applies equally to your use of technology and how you use only the devices and systems that extend your best abilities, relying on other skillful individuals to use other technologies. Every day, you strengthen what you do uniquely well by taking advantage of others' expanding technological mastery.

Dogs are actually a technology in the sense that there was no animal called the dog. It was a collaboration between human beings and social, adaptive wolves. And it's a technology that humans have been developing for 30,000 years. We're a technology-creating species. We take the natural world around us and transform it into useful things.

Establishing your relationship.
But in the same way that some people don't "get" dogs, they also don't get technology. This is because somehow they've allowed the dog or the technology to be in control of their life, and they find it annoying and burdensome. But we already know how to do this. We've spent millennia learning how to establish this relationship and make it work.

And the same rationale as it relates to dogs now relates to technology of all kinds: You have to establish who you are in relationship to the canines and to the technology. You have to own that you're the owner. That's how you're going to make both dogs and technology useful to you.

A lot of people feel they have to be up to date on every new technology. But these people are always scrambling because they're not owning the experience. The technology is owning them. You have to be clear about your individual skills and only use the technologies that leverage them.

Daily focus on growth.
You have significant external skills that others love to utilize. But your greatest inner talent is that you're always growing. Day after day, there is always measurable progress. This never ends because it's your greatest enjoyment. Anytime dogs are near you, they also love the energy that your never-ending growth communicates.

A talent for growth is a universal platform for every other talent. All nature responds to growth. The universe is all about growth, and there's a constant movement toward growth. And growth gets rewarded.

Surpassing your previous best.
You're very simple and uncomplicated in your daily progress. You always measure what your best results were yesterday, and surpass them today. Tomorrow, you'll improve even more. For dogs, this approach applied to their training is the best of all worlds and, equally, for your greater use of technology.

We may be the first people to refer to dogs as a technology, but I think that a particular approach to life created both dogs and what everyone refers to as technology. They come from the same mentality of creating useful things around us. A lot of people think there's something new happening in this "technological age." But as long as humans have been around, it's been the technological age. Fire, language, books—it's all technology.

We've always been utilizing things outside of ourselves to make life better and to better understand who we are, what we are, and where we're going. So the real difference between living 30,000 years ago and living today is that now we have all of that built-up technology at our disposal.

Being more yourself.

Because you're only striving to surpass who you uniquely were in the past, not competing with others, you keep getting better at who you're becoming. Every day, you have measurable new proof that you're more uniquely yourself. And the dogs in your life are always rewarded for the same thing. The only technologies you master follow the same rule of progress.

There's no cause for negative judgment of who you were at any point in the past. You've always done as well as was possible. If you judge who you were five years ago, imagine yourself judging who you are now five years down the road.

No comparing to others.

The more you appreciate who you uniquely are, the less you're tempted to be someone else. You never compare your progress to anyone else's. There's enormous freedom in this that expands outside of you. Dogs thrive in your growing uniqueness. And you only use the technologies that deepen and expand your best talents.

The outside world has become filled up with the creations of many, many innovators and inventors. We have a much more innovation-deep environment now than existed 10,000 years ago. The result is that there are many things outside of ourselves that can be tempting to use as a basis of comparison to ourselves.

But the only true measurement we can make of our progress is measuring back to where we were before. And using that measurement, we're always ahead of where we were. You can never walk around as somebody else, but you get information about who you are from your experience every day. All you have to do is put it in a coherent, consistent form of growth.

Only what you do uniquely.

You have a unique formula to daily life: You only deepen and expand what you do uniquely well, and you only apply your growing unique talent to collaboration with others who have the same commitment to unique value. The best dogs are those who are uniquely appreciated. The best technologies are those uniquely utilized.

You don't need to master every new technology. When it comes to technology, all you have to do is ask, "Does this help me to be more useful?" and "Does this improve my teamwork?" You're not going to spend any time working on something that you don't do well. You don't want to magnify weakness. You only want to magnify your unique strengths.

Chapter 4
Mindset 4: Deepening Your Values

You're increasingly clear about your fundamental lifetime values, and every year these values confidently guide your daily behavior.

Deep down, you're rock solid and becoming more so every day. You know who you are and what you stand for. This is especially important in today's world where many individuals are coming undone and are at loose ends. You have fundamentally permanent values that always get stronger, deeper, and more expansive in your relationship to each new day's experience.

Value is both a noun and a verb, and the two definitions are symbiotic, both applying to what has value in your life. Freedom is a central value of mine, and the freedom that I achieve is a function of how much freedom I allow other people to have. I want the people in my life to have the same freedom I enjoy because we learn from each other through our expanding freedom.

If you don't know what you value and can't comprehend how or why you might have personal value in other people's lives, then other people won't see any value in you either.

Lifetime fundamentals.
Right from the start, you've operated according to a solid understanding of what's right and wrong. Dogs immediately sense this—it's a source of comfort and confidence for them. Now that you're moving forward in the 21st century, all of your technological mastery is based on these same values.

Your understanding of what's right and wrong has come to you from experimenting in different situations and circumstances throughout your lifetime. You reach a point where you're set in your values, and so you don't have to experiment anymore. But you're still constantly on the lookout for new, better ways of doing things.

You've gathered a lot of information, but since you're always looking forward to things that are new, better, and different, you're always getting new information, and you're always testing out and refining the information you already have.

If you don't have any values, the sheer complexity of life in the 21st century will be overwhelming. If you're clear and confident about your values, you'll be cool and calm no matter what's happening in the outside world.

Consistent daily behavior.

Everyone who lives with you can count on you. You're positively predictable. Other people depend on your consistency for their own sense of daily capability and confidence. Dogs in your life get more useful because of your consistent daily behavior. Your use of technology multiplies your value in the world.

You're predictable in the sense that you're going to be positive and that you're going to aim to make situations positive. And you want everyone to get the benefit of that. No matter the situation, everyone who knows you knows that you'll be focused on making things better.

You look at the situation and figure out what you need to do and whether it's best if you switch direction. You're always ready to move forward in a positive way. You don't waste time wishing things were the way they were before. You're completely present, dealing with what's true in the moment.

Mastery of what you value.

There's a beautiful, growing impact that your consistent values create in all areas of your life. The dogs who are lucky to be around you take on this beauty. You improve them, and they increase your sense of enjoyment. From the start, all your reasons and strategies for using technology expand your deepest values.

Your expanding impact affects every area of your life—work, home, relationships, entertainment, travel, and so on.

When it comes to using technology, you have the choice: You choose how you use it, and you choose whether to use it in the first place. Just because something exists doesn't mean it's a fit for you and the life you want to lead.

For example, it's been five years since I completely gave up watching television in favor of spending my time doing more reading. And I haven't lost anything. I use only the technology that adds value to my life.

Clear, capable, and confident.

No matter how disruptive, complicated, and worrisome technology seems to many other people, for you it's always bringing greater clarity into your life. You're always becoming more capable and confident. You're always the owner of your technological engagement, the same as you are in your relationship with dogs.

Technology is only as disruptive as your own internal thinking. If your sense of your values is disruptive, confusing, and worrisome, you'll always be switching your values, and technology will be disruptive, confusing, and worrisome for you.

But you're decisive about what fits into your world and what doesn't, who fits into your world and who doesn't, and which technologies will serve you and which won't. That clarity is also appreciated by dogs. Having a clear, confident, and capable owner is much less stressful for them.

Inside-outside integrity.
For many technology users, the daily immersion in devices, systems, and networks confuses them about who they are, what they believe, and where they're heading. For you, it's uniquely different. Inside and outside, everything that makes you unique connects and grows with great technology.

There are always new things out there tempting you away from knowing who you are. This is because it's easier to manipulate people who don't know who they are. There are many people whose role in life is to convince people to buy things. I've been manipulated before, and it's never a positive experience.

The biggest protection you can have against manipulation is knowing who you are.

Chapter 5
Mindset 5: Increasing Your Usefulness

You've been useful to others from the very start, and every year, you find new ways to be even more useful — always helping others to get ahead.

Throughout your life, a single comment has most often been used to describe you: You're really useful. Different people at every stage of your life have said it, and they continue to say it now. It happens so often that you realize it's not actually about you so much as it is about their own experiences of making significantly easier progress when they're involved with you.

Dogs immediately show their appreciation for your usefulness, and when it comes to your use of technologies, you only use them to be more useful.

The way you find out who you are starts with being useful to somebody else. This connects the circuit, giving you a feedback loop from the outside world. And it's only once you've created value for someone else that you can expect any opportunity for yourself.

Useful from the start.
It seems to those who know you best that you came into the world being useful, both to yourself and to everyone who appreciates you. Dogs, encountering you for the first time, are attracted to you. And, because you're so useful, you choose to master only the most useful technologies to amplify your usefulness.

Your life really starts to make sense when you realize that your knowledge about what other people are after, and your ability to provide them with support and help, takes care of you for life. If you always show up looking for ways to be useful to other people, great things get said about you, you get referred to others, and doors open for you. And every time you're useful in moving someone forward, you know more about yourself. Being useful to others is the test of reality outside of yourself that proves what's inside of you.

The important questions to ask yourself are, "How can I be useful to someone else?," "What is it about me that's especially useful to other people?," and "To what kind of people am I especially useful?"

New, bigger, and better.
Every year now, there are new technological capabilities becoming available. You have an unerring sense in knowing which ones are useful for you and which ones to ignore. When you encounter dogs, they always behave in better ways. That's because everything about you involves new, bigger, and better experiences.

The entrepreneurial approach to a new technology is to do a fast, deep dive into whether it's useful for you. I knew the value of Zoom five years before we went in 100 percent on it. This is because before other people were using it, it wasn't useful. A telephone is only valuable if there's somebody else at the other end. So, I appreciated Zoom's usefulness, but recognized that it wasn't useful for me *yet*.

With the emergence of ChatGPT, I knew it was a clever technology, and I wondered if it would be useful. You have to be able to see what repetitive activity can be systematized and made automatic by the technology, thereby freeing up individuals for more creative work.

Helping others to improve.

There's a secret to your always-growing usefulness: You're always motivated to help others become more useful in their worlds. You improve yourself so that everyone you engage with is motivated to improve their usefulness. Dogs jump at the opportunity. And you only use technology to multiply your usefulness.

I made a fundamental decision that after I turned 70, all the growth I experienced would be teamwork growth, not individual growth. I'm good enough to be part of good teamwork. That's the only thing that's really necessary. And my seventies have been my most productive and creative decade yet. If you make each new decade more creative and productive than all your experience before that decade, you've got a neat little formula for growth and for ensuring that your future is always bigger than your past.

You may have your own ideas of why you're so useful. But it's other people's ability to be increasingly useful in their world as a result of you that's the proof of reality outside of yourself. This is where your uniqueness meets the world. Are you useful to them? Because that makes them more useful to other people.

They improve, you expand.

Your growing usefulness to others starts with your own endless passion for personal growth, greater capability, and increased confidence. But you recognized from the start that you had to be useful outside of yourself before the outside world of people, dogs, and technology could start being useful to you.

As far back as I can remember, I was always including other people in my world. I was aware of other people, and I was learning by asking them questions.

Part of your reality is the proof that you're making an impact outside of yourself. We all need that. It's like radar—you're sending out a signal and you get a bounce back. Our sense of reality about who we are grows with our sense of reality of our outside impact.

New technologies should never be treated like they're out of the norm of what human beings do. Creating technology is something human beings have always done. No new technology is going to change everything in the world; it's only going to change certain things. And the lasting value will be where it changes things for the better and makes you more useful.

Your head for getting ahead.

At all times, in all situations, in relationship to everyone and everything, you want to get ahead. This is because increasing growth feels good. Dogs feel it. Others who are similarly motivated feel it. And you have a great head here in the 21st century for owning and utilizing the right technologies that move everything ahead.

Your instincts for discernment get stronger and stronger. You learn to ask the right questions, like, "Who do I want to be?," "Who do I want to be useful to?," and "How can I be useful in the right way to the right people?" You're always getting better at figuring out what makes sense for you and what doesn't, including what technologies to adopt and in what way.

Chapter 6
Mindset 6: Multiplying Your Impact

Your productive use of technology is always multiplying its impact in the world because it's just one example of your increasing ownership of who you are.

Your technological ownership expands the territory of your unique personal impact. Your dog senses this and protects the territory they share with you, which continually grows, and your positive impact on everything you encounter constantly grows as well. It's a unique internal awareness and certainty that automatically expands outside of yourself.

Dogs, who are territorial by nature, immediately sense this and respond with their own growing confidence and capability. In very visible and measurable ways, they own and protect your territory.

Expanding territory.

To expand your territory, you have to be aware of and appreciate your impact in the world outside of yourself. Decades ago, Strategic Coach engaged entrepreneurs with a thinking tool called The Strategy Circle. If we hadn't appreciated the impact of that thinking tool, we never would have continually expanded our territory with hundreds more thinking tools as we did.

When it comes to using technology as a multiplier, you have to be completely aware of what you're multiplying. After all, you don't want to amplify negativity. You have to be a great person to be a great owner of technology and to have great uses for it. To get positive value out of technology, you have to work on yourself.

Danger of not taking ownership.

Ownership is vital. If someone never owns who they are or what they do, they never have any kind of ownership in the outside world around them. Lacking awareness, they have no certainty, which means they have no confidence— neither in the way they think about things nor in how take they action.

Everything about them lacks impact. Certainly, it lacks a positive impact. In fact, their involvement in any situation or circumstance depletes other people of their ownership. Dogs see them as so absent, they don't pay any attention to them. There's such a vast gap between them and the universe of any kind of useful technology that their "owning" it is unimaginable.

Each grows the other.

"Ownership" and "impact" multiply each other. The more you grow the one, the more it multiplies the other. You can see this clearly with your dog. As you grow, your dog is motivated to improve their usefulness. Your ownership of technology works the same way, continually multiplying your unique impact in the world.

In order to make great use of any technology, from a new app to dogs, you have to spend time making yourself great. For example, I don't produce better thinking tools for The Strategic Coach Program unless I'm using the tools to improve myself.

People who don't expand their territory are boring. And instead of owning, they're owned. They're trapped by some-thing in the past, and they're not creating anything new for the future. So, they end up with small territory that's old and uninteresting.

Certainty, confidence, impact.

Ownership multiplies conscious certainty. Certainty multiplies confidence. Confidence, in turn, multiplies the expanding territory of your impact in the world. Dogs love patrolling and protecting your relationship territory. Technology multiplies your ownership of "impact" territory in the world.

"Conscious" means that you know how it works—you know how to get it to work better, and you know how to get it to work differently.

A few years ago, when travel suddenly became impossible, we started using Zoom a lot more. This saved us an enormous amount of time, connecting us with people in one click instead of having to take a flight. We can see how using Zoom has vastly expanded our impact in the world, from virtual workshops to podcast recordings.

Everyone and everything.

Your impact in all of your relationships with the world is always multiplying because you're always increasing ownership of your entire life experience: past, present, and future. Everyone and everything that encounters you multiplies their unique usefulness because of your continually expanding ownership.

Mediocre human beings don't have great dogs or great technology. When there are great dogs and great uses of technology, that means there's a great human who's their owner.

Your goal is to be useful to other people. And so everything you do, including your use of technology, results in your capability enabling others.

Transformative impacts.

"Ownership" is the exact opposite of "being owned" when it comes to taking impactful action. Ownership action is increasingly confident and transformative. Always. "Being owned" leads to worried, hesitant, and deficient results. Always. Confident ownership multiplies transformative impact. Always.

Everything transformative is relationship-based. You have a relationship with people, you have a relationship with the world, you have a relationship with dogs, and you have a relationship with technology. And every one of your transformative relationships is always deepening. You use the capability of technology to magnify your relationship with the world.

If you're owned, the only action you take is the action you're allowed to take. As an owner, you can take whatever action you want. By definition, being an owner is less constrained.

You're free to be creative, and you can innovate new things that people will find valuable out in the world.

EVERYONE AND EVERYTHING...

Chapter 7
Mindset 7: Reversing Your Aging

You continually expand and strengthen daily fitness and health habits that reverse your aging one year every calendar year.

More and more, you're "owning" your physical existence. In other words, you're not hoping that you can keep going without working at it. In the past, you've taken your fitness and health for granted, but no more. They now have your full attention.

You're increasingly owning your physical future, with the result that you're getting biologically younger as you get chronologically older. The vast number of people your age are spending more of their time thinking about retiring from creativity and productivity. Some of them are already "retiring" and physically aging in their thirties. That's not you. You're always striving to be more successful.

If you want to always be expanding your territory, you can't be tired. You need to have a lot of highly focused energy in order to be ambitious, interested, and excited.

Getting younger.
Your ownership only expands in creative ways if you keep getting younger physically. Every year, you're energetically more fit. Your dog loves being around you because you're always in motion and doing new things. The most useful new technologies seem to be attracted to your creative energy.

There is greater possibility today than ever before to reverse your aging. And we have technology to thank for that.

Our eyes only see and our ears only hear what our brain is looking for. So if you're looking for a bigger future, you'll pick up on the technologies that will allow you to achieve that. The technologies that show up as being useful to you aren't the same ones that will show up for others. Each person is unique, and so are their capabilities, goals, and the technologies that will help them achieve them.

Growing your best ownership.
You've seen many examples of ownership in the world that are strictly the result of past creativity. More and more past—nothing new in the present. Your best-ever ownership is right now. Your ambitions are growing. Your dog is learning new tricks, and your best technologies are exponentially more powerful.

Certainty and commitment produce their own power and energy in the world. You can't be half committed and half certain. That's the same as not being committed and not being certain at all. It's like ownership of a company—there's a vast difference between owning 49% and owning 51%.

Your complete ownership isn't a destination, it's a way of being. You are always owning in the moment.

Three selves.
We have three selves: past, present, and future. And we only experience the present. We create our pasts by selectively choosing what to remember. And we're selective about how we want our futures to be.

The question is, "Are you using the past to build the future, or are you using the past to stop the future?" It's either create or stop. It takes no talent to have a past, only a heartbeat. But it does take talent to have a future.

Fear and excitement.

You're aware that all of your ownership growth so has far required equal amounts of fear and excitement. You had to commit to a bigger result before you had the capability to achieve it.

There are two sides of the growth coin. One is fear, which is there because you have to commit to the bigger result and be courageous before you can be capable and confident. When people want to retire, what they really want to retire from is experiencing fear. But without experiencing fear, you don't get to experience the other side of the growth coin, which is excitement. Fear and excitement are the two ingredients. You don't get one without the other.

Every year, your fear and excitement drive you to use technology in creative ways. This enables you to create unique value in a way that's faster, easier, cheaper, and has a bigger impact out in the world.

Surprising creativity.

You realize that you're playing a lifetime game of ownership with a permanently young mindset and approach. What's most exciting to you is the bigger surprises you're still creating and responding to.

Whether they're good or bad, all surprises are exciting because they present you with the opportunity to grow and learn.

Your dogs love surprises too. Whether it's a new treat, a new toy, or a new route to walk, surprises result in dogs becoming more creative and adventurous. And the bigger your ambition gets, the more technologies you'll find to serve it. More and more, technology seems to be custom-designed for your biggest ambitions.

But physical energy goes together with creative energy, which means you have to stay healthy and work hard in order to pull off your creative vision.

Best age reversal.

As you age chronologically, you're taking your biological age backwards by taking advantage of the best age-reversal breakthroughs. Twenty-five years ago, this wasn't even imaginable. Now, the best medicine is racing in this direction. It's what today's best technology is all about.

The technology's there to make things possible that used to seem like science fiction. You can also extend your dog's life and keep them healthy for their entire lifetime. And regenerative medicine will be a self-fulfilling prophecy: if enough people are interested in being young for longer, the necessary funds and technological developments will come along to support that goal. AI, for example, suddenly came into being when people's creative and productive aspirations required it.

Technology itself has no ambitions, plans, or purpose. It's driven by human aspiration, created by humans to serve *our* ambitions, plans, and purposes. This means we have to have aspirations in order for the technology to be created.

Chapter 8
Mindset 8: Slowing Life Down

You increase your daily ownership of your most useful lifetime habits in all areas of activity, both personal and business.

Your expanding ownership increases your enjoyable sense of everything slowing down. With expanding ownership, you automatically become more creative and productive. You discover more and more that you can't truly own anything outside of yourself unless you increasingly own what's inside of your mind and imagination.

It's like looking in the mirror at your life. What you see reflected back is all of the extraordinary value you're creating. Because you own more and more of that life, it's all there for you to see. Nothing's hurried, nothing's just flashing by.

Own your ownership.

Owning your capabilities is extended through technology, and dogs are a great example of technology. People don't have any problem accepting themselves as the owner of a dog, and the more you own your ownership, the better your relationship with the dog becomes.

But we treat technology as something different, and we don't take ownership of it the way we take ownership of dogs. Therefore, as new technologies are being created, we feel we have to keep up with them, and everything in life speeds up. All the things that speed up and surprise us and put us on edge are from our relationships with the technologies we don't actually own. In fact, we think they own us.

Productive daily habits.

You increasingly own all of your most creative and productive daily habits, and this enjoyably slows down every aspect of your life. You feel an increasing sense of clarity, confidence, and capability. All of your dogs are becoming great dogs. All of your technology is becoming great technology.

There aren't good habits and bad habits. There are successful habits and unsuccessful habits. The successful habits you increasingly own can affect all aspects of your life, from your health to your relationships to your peace of mind.

Your successful habits are stabilizing and reinforcing. And the more you engage in your creative and productive daily habits, the less energy they require. The predictability of your habits gives you a buffer against uncertain elements because you already know how much is certain. The outside, unpredictable world can't intrude on your habits.

Creativity speeds up.

Remarkably, as your great lifetime habits are slowing things down, your creativity and productivity speed up. That's because more of what you do every day creates new value. The more value you create, the more life slows down for you. And more value for your dogs and technology means slower time and life for you.

Your successful habits make you more creative. And because you can be more and more focused on what you're doing, you have intentional focus in every hour of your day. You're not being distracted from your purpose or from your intention.

When you're distracted, it uses up energy because you're taken away. Your focus is broken, and it takes a lot of energy to get back to the focus. Your increasing ownership of your habits means you're protected from things you don't own intruding and causing you to become distracted.

Others accelerating.

No matter what unpredictable factors are accelerating the lives of others, you're always slowing down. Technological innovation everywhere in the world is speeding up, but you're not. That's because you own every use of your own custom technology. And your dogs love every aspect of how you slow things down for them.

You're not jumping on the bandwagon for every new piece of tech. You're sorting it based on your own purposes and deciding what's specifically useful for *you*. Just because a new technology might be intriguing doesn't mean that it's useful for you. It's just a bright, shiny object.

If you're not clear on your intention and purpose, you're susceptible to being distracted by every new piece of technology. This means your time can get sucked away into a vortex, and you end up with something clever but not useful. You have to be able to slow down and discern what's worth your time to get involved with.

Delicious sense of time.

You increasingly have a delicious sense of owning more of your expanding life, with a growing sense of expanding time to enjoy every part of it. Everything you're enjoying the most, you're always expanding the time you have to do it.

If you're not enjoying your time, your experience of time speeds up because there's no pleasure in it for you to slow down and take it in. In my daily life, I never feel isolated or estranged. I'm not searching for something artificial to give myself a sense of connection. I'm always feeling the experience I'm in because I'm always enjoying the experience I'm in.

Always more useful.

Every time something usefully new emerges, you own it and integrate it with everything else that's already useful. Your time keeps growing more useful because you own more of it. Dogs benefit from having more of your enjoyable time. Your technology becomes exponentially more useful.

I live by the binary principle that if I'm not the owner, then I'm being owned. It's either one way or the other. You're either owning your own experience, or your experience is owned by something else. There's no middle ground.

To figure out if you're owning or being owned, there are great questions you can ask yourself: Why am I doing this? What purpose does this activity have? Am I better because of this? How does this fit into everything else I'm usefully doing? How does this make me more useful?

These are all ownership-enhancing questions because the answers you give provide a better way of thinking about these things than the way you'd been thinking before. And if you discover that you've been owned in an experience, you learn from that so it doesn't happen again, and in that way, you take ownership of it.

Conclusion
Works With Great People Too
Your ownership success with dogs and technology is a continually growing and rewarding experience that gets bigger and better.

And, surprise! This ownership thing spills over into everything else, especially your daily relationships with people and specifically with other "ownership" people. They're all around you. But you realize that you can't spot them until you take ownership of yourself. The more you're an owner— of dogs, technology, and everything else in your life—the more you'll attract and interact with other great owners.

Human beings either create or complain. People who don't take ownership of themselves are the complainers. They blame other people for their lack of enjoyment.

You are the common denominator in all your experiences. If you have purpose, you're going to recognize and attract other people with purpose. If you don't own who you are and what you're doing, you're always going to be frustrated. And you're only going to attract other frustrated people.

Other owners.
You may have been wondering if there's a punch line to this book. You may not have owned any dogs. You try to get by with a minimum of technology. There is a punch line. Dogs and technology are actually about ownership—about your ownership of who you uniquely are now and who you're becoming going forward.

The payoff for your ownership is that you get to meet other people who own themselves, who are always being increasingly creative and productive. This is what this whole book is really about. You're putting yourself in a position to attract, interact with, and collaborate with other great owners.

The difference between a successful entrepreneur and an entrepreneur who takes their impact to the next level is how much the entrepreneur has taken ownership of their life. At the higher level, there's no sense of scarcity, threat, or competition. For entrepreneurs who have complete ownership of their own lives, it's all about abundance, generosity, and sharing.

Collaborating at this level means you create brand new things and gain access to all sorts of skills from other people. Your enjoyment of your own life spills into everything you're involved in doing.

More capable and confident.

Dogs are a form of technology. Long-ago humans created dogs to improve survival and make greater progress. Both dogs and every other kind of technology are capabilities that make you more confident. They enable you to be more committed and courageous about being an even greater owner. It's an ongoing process and a lifetime recipe for always being creative and productive.

Becoming more capable and confident always involves a period of commitment and courage. Once you reach a higher level of capability and confidence, you take on greater commitments, and you're capable of greater courage to develop even greater capability and confidence.

If a human takes ownership of their relationship with a dog, it's now exponential what they can do compared to a human who isn't a great dog owner. The exact same is true for being a great owner of any kind of technology. And if you have a great purpose for a technology, your commitment and confidence about becoming an even better owner will grow.

Motivated to multiply.

Right now, you have capabilities you want to multiply. The best way to achieve this is by expanding your ownership of every area of your life. Thirty thousand years of humans owning dogs is a good, proven example of how useful technologies are created—and good evidence of the benefits of being a great owner.

Technology is a huge accelerator of our ambitions and practice. It always has been, even when the technology was much more primitive than it is today. When you apply your creativity and productivity to the technologies that best multiply them, you get a bigger result with less time and effort.

Creativity and productivity are great multipliers. They're emotionally thrilling. But they're not available to you until you take ownership of yourself.

Ingenious and resourceful.

Technology isn't a recent thing. You realize that other people have been doing this from the start. The history of humanity is the history of people being ever more ingenious and resourceful with everything around them. Dogs are a great example, then, of the ownership approach for every other technology.

Some people are automatically against adopting a new technology. The reason is that the results will be unpredictable, and they don't want anything to upset their old way of life. On the other hand, you and others who have taken complete ownership of yourselves and your capabilities will always be finding ways in which technology can magnify your capabilities.

What's more, you'll see ways that old resources can be useful again with the use of new technology even though others have dismissed the resources as being no longer useful. You know that humans are needed to make a resource valuable. And you know that the world we have today is the way it is because of all the innovations that humans have already made.

Ownership comes first.

Dog or no dog, you have plenty of technology to expand your unique ownership in the world. But ownership comes first, then technology. Then comes all of your collaboration with other owners.

Don't collaborate with non-owners. Collaborations with non-owners always fall apart and go sideways because when non-owners use technology, they make the technology wayward (e.g., "deepfakes"). Non-owners make bad guesses and bad bets, and technology magnifies these bad guesses and bad bets.

But as an owner yourself, you'll always be able to recognize when someone else is an owner, and so you'll be able to avoid getting into a collaboration with someone who isn't.

The Strategic Coach Program
Owning Your Four Freedoms
You now know that you want to own every aspect of your entrepreneurial life going forward.

You want greater freedom of your time, greater freedom of money, greater freedom of relationships, and greater freedom over your biggest and best purpose. You know this doesn't happen by some magic wand or miracle but by transforming your thinking.

You have a unique brain and powerful talents that produce remarkable results when they're focused. Strategic Coach is where you put them together. It's where everyone increasingly owns the four creative and productive freedoms that multiply every other reward of being an entrepreneur.

What makes entrepreneurs unhappy is when parts of their lives are owned or controlled by circumstances or other people. This could be due to regulations where they live or people they spend time with. All the obstacles that prevent someone from succeeding, enjoying themselves, and growing as an entrepreneur come from a lack of ownership in a particular area. But if you have ownership, you have control, and you're in charge.

Entrepreneurs are the only people who can achieve this because they've made a decision to take complete ownership of how they make money. You want to own every aspect of your entrepreneurial life going forward. This is possible, and Strategic Coach can help you do it.

Owning your time.
You master a complete time system that extends your ownership of every aspect of your past, present, and future,

both in your business and personal life. You're totally focused on what you most love doing.

Time is a measurement, but everyone experiences it differently. Your experience is 100 percent yours, and you can do anything you want with it. When people think of ownership, they usually think of tangible objects or other external things, but you can own what's inside too. This includes how you make up your past and your future. Strategic Coach has a system for entrepreneurs to own their time. And if you don't own your time, it will own you.

Owning your money.

With the right tools, you're able to deepen and expand your freedom of everything related to money. Your quality of money deepens, your quantity of money expands, and your use of money has greater impact.

Money is a byproduct of creating value. But, often, people don't emotionally own it. And not all money is equal. Strategic Coach clients learn how to make money so that it makes them happy, how to have a great purpose for making money, and how to gain financial freedom so they can pursue what they're passionate about.

Owning your relationships.

Ownership of time and money attracts your best relationships ever, in all areas. Other individuals with unique ownership qualities discover you, work with you, create with you, and collaborate with you in new ways.

The entire universe is held together by radio signals of a sort. If you're broadcasting on a particular frequency, other people who receive on that frequency are attracted to you. When people are isolated, it never goes well. At Strategic Coach, entrepreneurs who have taken ownership connect with other entrepreneurs who have taken ownership, and what each entrepreneur can accomplish increases exponentially through these relationships.

An entrepreneurial journey can only be launched in a solitary fashion. It's the decision of someone who has confidence in their uniqueness, that they can engage the marketplace head on. But that says nothing about your ability to connect with others and how vital doing so is for your success and happiness. The Strategic Coach Program helps you develop very high standards for who gets to connect with you.

Owning your purpose.
Ownership of time, money, and relationship create great purpose in your world, and you have immense persuasive impact in other owners' worlds.

The Four Freedoms are sequential as well as cumulative. Your freedoms of time, money, and relationship clearly identify what your big purpose is in life. And if you haven't recognized this already, you'll come to understand that retirement isn't a goal or a reward—it means retiring from your purpose. If retirement is your purpose, you have no purpose. What you want and what you can do is to continue doing what you do in a bigger and better way for the rest of your life.

The three levels of ownership freedom.
Strategic Coach provides you with a lifetime structure to increase your ownership and multiply your four entrepre-

neurial freedoms. The three levels that you climb are liberating from the start.

Entrepreneurs experienced in the use of Strategic Coach thinking tools continually grow upward and outward in their mastery of internal teamwork and external collaboration. They progress through the Signature, 10x Ambition, and Free Zone Frontier levels of the Program, using ever-more-powerful thinking tools.

The Signature Program frees you from friction and from anxious thinking related to status and competition. You become clear on the business life and personal life you want, you start expanding each of the Four Freedoms, and you build a Self-Managing Company.

Eventually, you realize it's easier to plan for 10x progress than it is to try to push the existing system further by working harder and longer. In **The 10x Ambition Program**, you build on your self-managing foundation and start creating a self-multiplying foundation.

Then you're ready to enter a society where everybody has reached a higher stage of thinking and development. And that's **The Free Zone Frontier Program**. Every entrepreneur in the Free Zone is at the top of their game. They've left status concerns behind, they operate with abundance mindsets, and they're ready to collaborate and grow their impact at the very highest levels.

For more information and to register for The Strategic Coach Program, call 416.531.7399 or 1.800.387.3206, or visit us online at *strategiccoach.com*.

THREE LEVELS OF

FREE ZONE

Your own 10x personal and 10x company growth continually transform within an expanding global community of other Self-Multiplying Companies. These entrepreneurs are increasingly bypassing all competition in their industries and markets by creating 10x up to 1,000x collaborations that will grow in IP asset value to US$15 trillion by 2044.

10X AMBITION

With your increasingly productive and profitable Self-Managing Company, your personal ambition confidently envisions 10x growth in all areas of your business and personal life — certainly within a 10-year period. As this 10x Mindset permeates throughout everyone's daily teamwork, the entire organization becomes a Self-Multiplying Company.

SIGNATURE

You identify and establish your Unique Ability as the dynamic center of your business and personal life. This enables you to create a constantly expanding Self-Managing Company in which all team members grow in their creativity, productivity, and collaboration. Your personal income and Free Days increase, and you plan to never retire.

About The Author
Dan Sullivan

 Dan Sullivan is the founder and president of The Strategic Coach Inc. and creator of The Strategic Coach® Program, which helps accomplished entrepreneurs reach new heights of success and happiness. He is author of over 50 publications, including *The Great Crossover, The 21st Century Agent, Creative Destruction, How The Best Get Better*, and The Ambition Series of quarterly small books. He is co-author of *Who Not How, The Gap And The Gain, 10x Is Easier Than 2x, The Laws of Lifetime Growth*, and *The Advisor Century*.